MW01104793

Seesaw

Vancouver based writer and director, Dennis Foon is known both nationally and internationally for his contribution to innovative theatre for young people. In 1989 he received the International Arts for Young Audiences Award in recognition of his work. His many plays, which have been produced extensively throughout Canada and the world (translated into French, Danish, Hebrew and Cantonese), include *The Short Tree and the Bird that Could Not Sing* (Chalmers Award), *Invisible Kids* (British Theatre Award), *New Canadian Kid, Mirror Game* (Blizzard), *Skin* (Chalmers Award, Governor General's Finalist), and *War* (Blizzard). Dennis was co-founder of Vancouver's Green Thumb Theatre where he was Artistic Director from 1975 to 1987. His screenplay, *Little Criminals*, is being produced by CBC-TV as a television feature film.

Seesaw

by
Dennis Foon

Blizzard Publishing • **Winnipeg**

Seesaw first published 1993 by
Blizzard Publishing Inc.
73 Furby Street Winnipeg, Canada R3C 2A2
© 1993 Dennis Foon
Reprinted 1995

Cover design by Scott Barham
Printed in Canada by Friesen Printers.

Published with the assistance of
the Canada Council and the Manitoba Arts Council.

Caution

All photos © Hubert Pantel. Photos are from the première production of
Seesaw by Manitoba Theatre for Young People, February 1993.
Canadian Cataloguing in Publication Data

Foon, Dennis, 1951–
    Seesaw
    A play.
    ISBN 0-921368-35-6
I. Title.
PS8561.062S4 1993   jC812'.54   C93-098123-5
PR9199.3.F66S4 1993

Seesaw was first produced by Manitoba Theatre for Young People at the Gas Station Theatre, Winnipeg, February 5, 1993, with the following cast:

JOSH	Robert Slade
CHARLA	Jan Skene
ADAM	Chris Sigurdson
PAIGE	Monique Marcker

Directed by Richard Greenblatt
Designed by Ronnie Burkett
Music by Cathy Nosaty
Lighting by Larry Isacoff
Stage Managed by Carolyn Kutchyera

Seesaw was commissioned by Manitoba Theatre for Young People (MTYP), Leslee Silverman, Artistic Director. It was first workshopped at the Banff Playwrights Colony in the spring, 1991. It was subsequently workshopped in Vancouver by The New Play Centre with the support of MTYP and Green Thumb Theatre. Many thanks to these organizations and the workshop participants for their invaluable assistance.

Particular thanks to my collaborators, Richard Greenblatt (Director) and Ronnie Burkett (Designer), who were part of the developmental process of *Seesaw* through the workshop and production stages. Our goal over this long process was to collectively discover a visual vocabulary for the play, a journey that was incalculably enriched by their great commitment and fabulous imaginations.

I am also grateful to Elizabeth Dancoes for suggesting the play's title.

Playwright's Note

I began working on *Seesaw* by talking with seventy-eight sixth and seventh graders from a wide range of schools in Winnipeg. When I started, I did not know what I was going to write about. By the time I finished talking to them, the themes of the play became very clear to me. The students I spoke to came from many different kinds of environments. Some came from very tough homes, others came from very privileged ones, but all of them were struggling with huge emotional forces. The situations they faced outside their homes were becoming more and more aggressive and filled with conflict. At the same time, they were getting less and less help and support at home because their parents were often wrapped up in the basics of working and earning a living.

In *Seesaw*, I wanted to capture the feeling of walking on a tightrope these kids experience. I wanted to show the forces many twelve-year-olds keep in balance in order to survive. There is no seesaw in this play, but in every scene you can see which character is "on top" and which character is "at the bottom" and watch how the balance keeps changing. To have fun on a seesaw both people must co-operate, but if one person suddenly jumps off their end, the other person falls to the ground and gets hurt.

One very big part of kids' lives is television, the media and consumerism. In this play there are endless references to television shows, media stars, popular places to shop and more that quickly become dated. For example, when I first wrote this play, Paige's role model was the movie actress Julia Roberts; in this edition it is the super-model Claudia Schiffer. By the time you read this, I'm sure Claudia will be passé. Whenever this play is performed every effort should be made to find up to the minute replacements for references like these that inevitably become dated. In this book, many of these references to popular "flavours of the month" are enclosed in square brackets, [like this], so that you can substitute new names as you read.

The kids I spoke to were smart, talented, and optimistic. They all had big dreams and great hopes for the future, despite the uncertainty. They moved me and filled me with hope. This play is for them.

Dennis Foon

The cast of Manitoba Theatre for Young People's première of *Seesaw*, from left to right, Robert Slade as JOSH, Jan Skene as CHARLA, Monique Marcker as PAIGE, and Chris Sigurdson as ADAM.

Characters

JOSH
CHARLA
PAIGE
ADAM
They are all in grade seven.

Puppets

All the other characters are played by animated objects, puppets, masked figures or voices. They include:

TV
MISHA, Paige's half-brother
MOM, Paige's mother
DAD, Paige's stepfather
ANNE, Josh's mother
BILL, Josh's father
ELLEN, Charla's mother
MICKY
ZEDNIK
NYTRO
CAT, Adam's mother
DOG, Adam's stepfather

Most of the puppets are described in the text; directors and casts are encouraged to explore creative ways of realizing these characters. The following notes describe some of the approaches taken by the original production.

I describe Josh's parents in the play as an "attaché case" and a "telephone." In the original production, we decided not to make these two characters puppets. The actors wore head pieces that allowed a clear view of their faces. BILL had a visor that he snapped down when he went into business mode and carried a cellular phone; ANNE had a spinning wheel that had her appointments clipped to it and carried an attaché case that contained a heart, a Nintendo game and Josh's lunch money.

MISHA was a two-foot-high doll with a spinning head that had two faces: one angelic, the other demonic, complete with pointed teeth and horns. Paige's parents only saw his angelic side. Paige, of course, was constantly exposed to the demon.

The actors playing ADAM, CHARLA, PAIGE and JOSH each carried a hand puppet that represented their "secret" or "inner" self. In moments of hurt, loneliness or fear they put on the hand puppet and comforted it.

The play may be performed by as few as four actors. However, the final scene with NYTRO may require an "assist" by the stage manager.

The Set

The play takes place in many different locations but the only stage-requirement is a large "brick" wall masking the upstage area.

Covered in graffiti, the wall is the place where Adam goes to draw his bird, the eagle that eventually emerges from behind the bricks.

This wall also provides Nytro a place to "crash" through and a position (at the top of the wall) for the operators to control the human Ellen in her last scene with Charla.

In the original production, four cubes were used to create all the different environments. For example, the top of an overstuffed chair sat on one of the cubes to represent Adam's house. The back of the chair had the house's exterior painted on it and when this side faced the audience it represented the front porch of Adam's house. When the chair was turned around to face the audience, it represented the inside of Adam's house. Adam sat in the chair and the dog and cat fought on the overstuffed arms.

Act One

(Lights come up one at a time on ADAM, PAIGE, JOSH and CHARLA. Each is in his or her own area, in front of a TV, flipping through the channels with a remote.

Note: We do not actually see the TV sets. The actors' actions and the sounds of TV shows make this clear.

First we meet ADAM. When the lights come up on him he is playing a video game. He gives a shout of victory.)

ADAM: One hundred thousand twenty six—whatta score!

(ADAM stands triumphantly and hits the remote. We hear sounds of a martial arts battle.)

TV: What'd you call me? What? Are you holding out on me?

(Sounds of fighting.)

ADAM: [Van Damme] kicks butt!

(He picks up a piece of paper, studies it, draws something on it with his pencil and shoves it in his pocket. He does some karate kicks and punches.)

Weapons of death! Let the blood spill!

(He exits with his school bag.

Lights come up on PAIGE, who is flipping channels with her remote. She stops on a version of [Entertainment Tonight].)

TV: ... and speaking of boyfriends, how 'bout that [Claudia Schiffer]—

PAIGE: [Claudia Schiffer]!

TV: [Claudia's] latest fling is the Prince of Morocco!

PAIGE: He's cute!

TV: And what do you think of her new hairstyle?

PAIGE: I love it!

(PAIGE brushes her hair to look like [Claudia's].

Enter MISHA, PAIGE's little brother and a puppet. He grabs the remote.)

MISHA: I wanna watch [Muppet Babies].

(PAIGE grabs back the remote.)

PAIGE: No, Misha!

MISHA: Paige! Gimmee it Paige!

(She holds it over his head. He unsuccessfully jumps for it.)

PAIGE: Get outta here, Misha, go bug your Daddy!

MISHA: He's your Daddy too!

PAIGE: He is not! Get out!

MISHA: No!

(MISHA's face turns devilish. He bites PAIGE's leg.)

PAIGE: Ow!

(She drops the remote. MISHA hits the button. The [Muppet Babies'] theme comes on. PAIGE grabs the remote back, turns off the TV. MISHA cries.)

MISHA: No fair, Paige, no fair!

PAIGE: You bit me!

(MISHA kicks PAIGE.)

You little brat!

(PAIGE raises her hand to hit him, he cries.)

MISHA: Mommy, Mommy! Paige hit me!

(Enter Paige's MOM, a giant mannequin, and DAD, her stepfather, who is a posh sportscar.

MISHA puts on an angelic face.)

MOM: Paige, leave your brother alone!

PAIGE: I didn't do anything!

DAD: You must have done something.

PAIGE: He bit me and kicked me!

DAD: He's just trying to show you affection.

PAIGE: *(To MISHA.)* I love you, too.

(PAIGE pinches MISHA, who cries.)

MISHA: Mommy—Daddy!!

MOM/DAD: Paige!

(PAIGE exits.

Lights come up on JOSH, who is lying in front of his TV, watching a rock video. He does not react to the lively music.

His mother, ANNE, enters. She is an attaché case.)

ANNE: Good morning!

(JOSH turns down the TV.)

JOSH: Hi, Mom.

ANNE: All ready for school, Josh?

JOSH: I have a stomach ache.

ANNE: That's the third day in a row.

JOSH: I better stay home.

(His father, BILL, enters. He is a telephone.)

BILL: See you later, I gotta go.

ANNE: Me too, I'm really late.

BILL: You better get ready, Josh.

JOSH: I don't feel good.

BILL: You'll be fine. I gotta go.

ANNE: Home for dinner?

BILL: No, sorry, I have a meeting.

ANNE: Me too.

BILL: I'll phone.

(BILL exits.)

ANNE: Now come on, Josh, let's go, I'm gonna be late.

JOSH: I need lunch money.

ANNE: Sure, sure, help yourself.

(JOSH reaches into the attaché case and takes a two dollar bill.)

Let's have a hug.

(JOSH reaches into the attaché case, takes out a small plush heart and hugs it.)

I've got an eight forty five. Step on it!

(JOSH puts back the heart. She exits, JOSH follows.

Lights come up on CHARLA.

Her mother, ELLEN, enters. She is a marionette. The operator controlling her is dressed like the marionette and is visible to the audience.)

ELLEN: Your lunch is still in the fridge, Charla.

CHARLA: I won't forget it.

ELLEN: Did you have milk this morning, Charla?

CHARLA: There was only half a glass.

ELLEN: I'll get more after work. You drink two glasses when I get home, okay?

CHARLA: 'kay.

ELLEN: … Is something wrong?

CHARLA: What do you think?

ELLEN: … First day of school?

CHARLA: A new one. They're gonna kill me.

ELLEN: That's exactly how I feel about my new job. What are they going to think of me? What if they think I stink?

CHARLA: You're not gonna stink.

ELLEN: Neither are you.

CHARLA: Then why's my stomach feel like World War Three?

ELLEN: Let's both try taking a deep breath.

(They both do. ELLEN exhales. CHARLA continues holding hers. Long pause. She starts turning blue.)

Charla? Charla, you have to breathe!

(CHARLA gasps.)

Are you alright?

CHARLA: I don't know anybody. How'm I supposed to make friends?

ELLEN: It happens. But don't push it. You don't just need friends. You need the right friends … Where are my keys? I just had them—

CHARLA: Right here, Mom.

ELLEN: Thanks. Let's go.

(CHARLA and ELLEN exit.

JOSH enters, furtively. He sees ADAM enter and hides.

ADAM pulls his piece of paper out of his pocket and looks at it. He takes out his pencil and carefully makes adjustments on it. Then he writes something on it, thinks about it and crosses it out.

CHARLA enters. ADAM sees her, pockets the paper and then goes to her.)

ADAM: Who are you?

CHARLA: Charla. Who are you?

ADAM: None of your business, Charcoal.

CHARLA: My name's Charla.

ADAM: What's in the bag, Charcoal?

CHARLA: None of your business.

ADAM: Lemmee see.

(ADAM grabs her bag and starts to reach into it.)

CHARLA: No way.

(CHARLA grabs it back.

ADAM smiles and wiggles his finger at her.)

ADAM: Kootchie kootchie koo.

(PAIGE enters.

ADAM runs to her.)

Hi Paige.

PAIGE: Hi Adam.

ADAM: Wanna pack of gum?

PAIGE: No thanks.

ADAM: Here.

(He gives it to her. She accepts it. He kisses her. She slaps him. They smile.)

PAIGE: You're a pervert, Adam. You're gross.

(JOSH starts to sneak off. ADAM sees him.)

ADAM: Where're you goin', Josh?

JOSH: In ... inta school.

ADAM: You didn't even say hi to me. Don't you say hello?

JOSH: Hello.

ADAM: *(Poking him.)* Hello, what?

JOSH: Hello, Adam.

ADAM: *(Shoving him.)* What did you call me?

JOSH: Adam.

ADAM: Did I say you could call me that?

JOSH: No.

ADAM: Then why'd you say it?

JOSH: I don't know.

ADAM: What?

JOSH: I don't know.

ADAM: What?

JOSH: I don't know.

ADAM: What?

JOSH: I don't know.

CHARLA listens while ADAM bullies JOSH.

(*ADAM shoves JOSH several times, pushing him out of earshot of the girls.*)

ADAM: You wanna live?

JOSH: Yes.

ADAM: Then whattaya got for me today?

(*JOSH reaches into his pocket, gives ADAM the two dollar bill.*) Is that all?

JOSH: Uh huh.

ADAM: Are you holding out on me?

JOSH: No.

(*ADAM squeezes JOSH's face.*)

ADAM: You better not be, Wimpsucker.

(*ADAM throws JOSH on the ground and struts away, smiling at the girls. PAIGE is not impressed. CHARLA runs over to JOSH.*)

CHARLA: Are you okay?

(*JOSH gets up. CHARLA hands him his school pack. JOSH takes it and runs off.*)

PAIGE: I'm Paige. Are you new here?

CHARLA: First day. I'm Charla. What's with that Adam?

PAIGE: Oh, he does that to everybody but especially Josh. He steals too—did you see him try to kiss me?

CHARLA: Yeah.

PAIGE: He's not the only one. Kim tried to kiss me yesterday. He said he wants to be my boyfriend—I told him to stick his head in the toilet. Roy was my boyfriend from February to May but I broke up with him 'cause he ate too much pizza.

CHARLA: Too much pizza?

PAIGE: The tomato sauce gave him a red moustache, it was gross—do you have a boyfriend?

CHARLA: No.

PAIGE: My boyfriend is Micky.

(*MICKY enters. He is a trendily dressed, boy mannequin on wheels. An operator works his arms.*)

He's the cutest boy in the whole school. He even did a TV commercial he's so cute. And met [Kirsty Alley] and gave me her autograph.

(MICKY goes to PAIGE and holds her hand.)

I love the presents he gives me.

(MICKY hands PAIGE some pencils and puts a ring on her finger.)

And he gave me his ring to wear. Don't you love it? I know some people who would kill for it. But he gave it to me ... I don't mind kissing Micky 'cause we're in love.

(PAIGE kisses MICKY. CHARLA is embarrassed. MICKY exits.)

Everybody says he's the most popular boy in school and I'm the most popular girl. Do you think that's true? Of course, you wouldn't know, you just got here.

CHARLA: I haven't even been to class yet.

PAIGE: We have a group, you know. Of really special people. We go skating together and to the mall. Wanna be in it?

CHARLA: Sure.

PAIGE: Okay. I'll talk to everybody. I mean it's really my decision and everything but I have to keep it fair, you know what I mean?

CHARLA: Yeah.

PAIGE: So I'll let you know, okay?

CHARLA: Okay.

(As PAIGE exits, she waves to a friend.)

PAIGE: Hi!

(CHARLA watches her go.

The school bell rings. All four kids take their places for class. ADAM comes in last. Before he sits, he goes to JOSH and smacks him on the head.)

ADAM: Get outta my seat.

JOSH: The teacher put me here.

ADAM: Well who's in charge, me or him?

JOSH: ... He's the teacher.

(ADAM smacks JOSH again.)

ADAM: Who's your boss?

(JOSH moves to the next seat.)

Good very good. You get a star.

(ADAM snaps his finger in JOSH's face.

ADAM sits in a different seat, leaving JOSH's original place empty. ADAM takes out his piece of paper and draws on it.

Mr. ZEDNIK, unseen by the audience, enters the classroom. All four kids sit up straight.

They perform ZEDNIK's voice in unison. When speaking his voice, they look down at their desks; when speaking directly to ZEDNIK they look up.)

ZEDNIK: Good morning class.

ALL: Good morning Mr. Zednik.

ZEDNIK: We have a new student in our class. I'd like you all to welcome Charla Williams. Josh?

JOSH: Yes, sir?

ZEDNIK: Why aren't you sitting in your correct place?

JOSH: I …

ZEDNIK: Well, move.

(JOSH quickly moves back into his original place.)

Now. Your book presentations. Who would like to go first?

(PAIGE eagerly holds up her hand.)

Alright, Paige.

PAIGE: My report is on the autobiography of [Claudia Schiffer]. From the moment she was born, everybody knew she was going to be a superstar because she was such a perfect baby and didn't cry at all.

(ADAM pokes JOSH with his pencil. JOSH moves over in his seat to get away.)

Did you know that [Claudia Schiffer's] hair grows faster than normal people's? Her hair was rated the most perfect by the Hairdressers Association of North America.

(ADAM pokes JOSH again with his pencil. JOSH moves away but this time falls off his chair.)

ZEDNIK: Josh, are you okay?

JOSH: Yes, sir.

ZEDNIK: What happened?

JOSH: I … I slipped.

ZEDNIK: Adam?

ADAM: Yes, sir?

ZEDNIK: Did you push Josh?

ADAM: No, sir.

ZEDNIK: Did you poke him?

ADAM: With what, sir?

ZEDNIK: You tell me.

ADAM: No way I could reach him from my seat, sir. Besides, all I got is my eraser in my hand and that wouldn't poke him very well, do you think, sir?

ZEDNIK: Alright then, get your notebooks out for a dictation exercise.

(As they pull out their notebooks, ADAM folds up the piece of paper he's been working on and passes it to CHARLA, indicating that she should give it to PAIGE. CHARLA does.)

What are you doing, Charla?

CHARLA: Getting out a notebook, sir.

ZEDNIK: Very good, Charla. Pencils ready? The first sentence is: Blah blah blah blah blah blah.

(The bell rings. The kids run out.

JOSH sits by himself. CHARLA starts to go to him but is stopped by PAIGE.)

PAIGE: How'd you like my book report?

CHARLA: It was interesting.

PAIGE: I should hope so, I made it all up.

CHARLA: You did?

PAIGE: Yeah! I didn't have to read a book. I heard something about her hair on TV. And that stuff about the baby? That's what they said about me, when I was born. Perfect baby. Didn't cry. Superstar. What'd they say about you?

CHARLA: I don't remember.

(PAIGE reaches into her pocket.)

PAIGE: Oh, right, Adam's note.

(She opens it.)

What is this?

CHARLA: It's a drawing.

PAIGE: It's weird.

CHARLA: It's nice.

PAIGE: You're weird. What does it say?

CHARLA: It's crossed out. It says—I ... love you.

PAIGE: Lemmee see that. *(She giggles.)* What a goof.

(She throws it on the ground.)

CHARLA: Don't you want it?

PAIGE: Are you kidding? It's got germs. Did you see the new [Vogue]?

CHARLA: No.

(PAIGE pulls it out, points at the cover.)

PAIGE: I love that colour on her.

CHARLA: It would look good on you too.

PAIGE: You think so?

CHARLA: That shade of blue's perfect for you.

PAIGE: Maybe if I grew my hair.

CHARLA: I was thinking about growing mine too.

PAIGE: I'm gonna perm mine like hers.

CHARLA: That'd look great.

PAIGE: You should perm yours too.

(MICKY enters.)

Micky!

(MICKY holds up his wrist. He is wearing a watch.)

What's that? A Rolex! *(To CHARLA.)* His uncle gave him a real Rolex for his birthday! *(To MICKY.)* Is that your uncle who lives in Hollywood? The one who helped produce [Terminator Two]?

(MICKY pulls out his date book.)

A birthday party? I think it'd be great at your house. Musicman for DJ? Perfect, he's the best. Printed invitations? Good idea.

(She starts making a list.)

Who should we invite? Boys: Sean, Jason, Justin, Ben, Chris, Alex ...

(She looks at JOSH, who's immersed in a Gameboy. She facetiously motions to MICKY, as if to say, "Should we invite him?" She giggles, then back to her list.)

Brent, Chad, Jake. Girls: Catherine, Julia, Tuesday ...

(CHARLA watches PAIGE hopefully.)

Michelle, Melissa, Emily, Sara, Rebecca ...

(MICKY makes a point.)

No, Micky, not Allison M, she's boring. Stephanie, Kristen, Kimberly ...

(PAIGE looks at CHARLA as she tries to think of the last name. CHARLA is on the edge of her seat hoping.)

Monica! I think that's everybody. Okay, let's go ... see you later, Charla.

CHARLA: Bye.

(CHARLA sadly watches PAIGE and MICKY go. PAIGE turns, calling back to CHARLA.)

PAIGE: Call me!

CHARLA: What's your number?

(PAIGE exits.

CHARLA picks up the note, looks at it, carefully folds and pockets it, goes to JOSH.)

Hi.

JOSH: Hello.

CHARLA: I saw what Adam did to you in class today.

JOSH: What did he do?

CHARLA: He was stabbing you with his pencil.

JOSH: Yes, that's correct.

CHARLA: Why didn't you say anything?

JOSH: About what?

CHARLA: About what Adam did to you.

JOSH: I couldn't do that.

CHARLA: Why not?

JOSH: Because if I tell, my nose might break.

CHARLA: That's terrible.

JOSH: When your nose breaks, the blood completely ruins your mathematics homework. Hide!

(JOSH hides. CHARLA follows.

ADAM enters. ADAM looks around. Satisfied he is alone, ADAM checks the chain on a bike. He takes a screwdriver out and breaks the lock. He jumps on the bike and rides off.)

CHARLA: Did you see what he did?

JOSH: Yes.

CHARLA: That was somebody's bike.

JOSH: Not any more.

CHARLA: He stole it.

JOSH: He'll take it apart and sell the pieces.

CHARLA: He could get arrested for that.

JOSH: Oh yes, he's been arrested before. He doesn't like the police.

CHARLA: Then why does he do it?

> *(We hear a menacing sound.*
>
> *NYTRO appears. He is a gigantic hand who bursts through the wall.)*

NYTRO: How long you been standing there?

JOSH: Just a couple minutes, Nytro.

NYTRO asks JOSH about the missing bike.

NYTRO: There was a bike here.

JOSH: All the bikes are gone now, Nytro. All the kids went home.

NYTRO: My little brother's bike was here but now it's missing.

JOSH: Maybe he took it home.

NYTRO: Maybe somebody lifted it.

CHARLA: I think ...

> *(JOSH kicks CHARLA.)*

NYTRO: What?

CHARLA: Nothing.

NYTRO: Well if you find something out, tell me. I'm at the high school across the street.

CHARLA: Okay.

JOSH: We'll be sure to let you know.

NYTRO: Stay healthy, kids. Are you drinking three glasses of milk everyday?

JOSH: Yes, Nytro.

NYTRO: Good.

> *(They watch him go.)*

CHARLA: Why not tell him the truth?

JOSH: Because of four broken noses.

CHARLA: Pardon me?

JOSH: Nytro goes to Adam, Adam fakes him out, Nytro comes back, breaks our noses for lying. Then, Adam finds us and breaks our noses again for telling. This way, instead of four broken noses, we got none.

CHARLA: What grade is Nytro in?

JOSH: Grade ten.

CHARLA: He's scary.

JOSH: Yes. But he was in a good mood.

CHARLA: You call that a good mood?

JOSH: He didn't take any money or even hit us once.

CHARLA: Must be our lucky day.

JOSH: Yes. It must be. Our lucky day.

> *(JOSH runs off. CHARLA exits.*

ADAM enters with the bike, he hides it on the side. He knocks on the front door of his house.)

ADAM: Hello? Mom.

(He bangs loudly.)

Mom!

(He tries the door again. It's locked.)

Mom!

(ADAM curls up in front of his house alone.

PAIGE enters. Her mother is touching up her make-up.)

PAIGE: I did my oral report today, Mom.

MOM: Hand me my earrings, Darling.

PAIGE: The teacher said it was excellent.

MOM: Excellent! That's wonderful, Paige. What were you wearing?

PAIGE: This.

MOM: You stood up in front of the whole class wearing that outfit?

PAIGE: You don't like it?

MOM: No, it's fine. Very presentable.

PAIGE: You hate it.

MOM: Well, your [Esprit] top is better with the [Guess] jeans.

PAIGE: They were dirty.

MOM: Then that's that. Did you see Micky today?

PAIGE: Yes, he got a Rolex from his uncle for his birthday.

MOM: A Rolex! From the uncle who works with [Arnold Schwartznager]?

PAIGE: Yes! And Micky's throwing a major birthday party and I'm helping plan it!

MOM: Fantastic! Paige, that's incredible! What are you going to wear?

PAIGE: Not this.

MOM: No, you'll need a new outfit.

PAIGE: When will we go?

MOM: You go, I'll give you my credit card.

PAIGE: Thank you, Mom.

MOM: Hand me my eyeliner ... I saw Micky in that [Bay] commercial. He's going to be a very big star. He's got the looks and the connections.

PAIGE: Isn't he the cutest?

MOM: Very [Christian Slater].

   (MISHA enters, a bra on his head.)

MISHA: Mommy, Mommy, I can't see!

PAIGE: Get that off, you brat!

MOM: *(Laughs.)* Look at him! Can you believe it!

PAIGE: He's got my bra on his head!

   (Flushed, PAIGE grabs it from him.)

MISHA: Give it back! My hide and seek mask!

PAIGE: I told you to stay out of my room!

MOM: Oh come on, Paige, don't you have a sense of humour?

MISHA: I want my mask!

MOM: Go on, give it to him.

PAIGE: It's my underwear.

PAIGE with her MOM and her little brother MISHA.

MOM: Oh, come on, you can buy another one at the mall.

(MOM exits.

MISHA's face turns devilish just for PAIGE. He chuckles. PAIGE throws the bra in MISHA's face and exits.)

MISHA: Ha!

(JOSH watches television as he works on a magic trick.)

TV: And now, Video Magician, take the wand, tap your hand three times ...

(JOSH does.)

Say the incantation ...

JOSH: Incastapa quo bohanti

TV: And reveal the magic cloth.

(JOSH pulls a square of silk cloth out of his sleeve. He smiles.)

And now Video Swandini will demonstrate the greatest feat of all: Invisibility.

JOSH: Invisible.

TV: Take the cloth and say the incantation ...

JOSH: Incastapa quo bohanti

TV: Place the cloth over the subject ...

(JOSH covers himself with the silk.

His parents, the attaché case and telephone, enter.)

ANNE: Josh?

BILL: Sorry we're back so late, son. I'm trying to close this deal.

JOSH: Can you see me?

ANNE: I sold three units today, Josh. That means more video games for you.

JOSH: I'm invisible.

ANNE: The more money I make, the more toys for the love of my life.

BILL: I've got an idea, why don't we read a book together, or play a game?

(JOSH removes the cloth.)

JOSH: Yeah, yeah! I've got a game we can play!

ANNE: Great, darling, let's go!

(JOSH pulls out a game.

The phone rings.)

BILL: *(Into the phone.)* Hello? They want six and a quarter? I said six!

ANNE: Oh, Josh, while your Dad's on the phone I'll just work on some stuff. I won't be a minute, darling.

BILL: *(To JOSH.)* Josh, be right there! *(Into the phone.)* Six, I said six!

(ANNE and BILL exit.)

TV: Alright, my friend, did it work? Are you invisible?

JOSH: Incastapa quo bohanti. Invisible!

(And JOSH throws the cloth back over his head.

CHARLA enters. She is making something with string. Her mother, the marionette, enters.)

ELLEN: I'm sorry I'm late, my new boss asked me to put in overtime on my first day and I was stuck. I'll start dinner. What are you making, Charla?

JOSH hopes to play with his mother and father.

CHARLA: A wish bracelet.

ELLEN: For who?

CHARLA: A girl in my class. Paige.

ELLEN: A new friend! That's great, is she nice? Who's the other one for?

CHARLA: Me.

ELLEN: Are you wishing for something?

CHARLA: Yes.

ELLEN: What are you wishing for?

CHARLA: For Dad to come home.

(CHARLA pulls on ELLEN's strings, stopping her.)

ELLEN: But he's not Charla. You won't see him again till summer.

CHARLA: That stinks.

ELLEN: I know, I'm sorry about what's happened, Charla, I really am.

CHARLA: That makes two of us.

ELLEN: I wish there was something I could do.

CHARLA: Can we go to a football game?

ELLEN: You and me?

CHARLA: Yeah, we never do anything.

ELLEN: But a football game—

(CHARLA grabs ELLEN's strings again.)

CHARLA: Dad used take me all the time.

ELLEN: *(Appalled.)* I know.

CHARLA: It's not just gross, it's fun. We liked it.

ELLEN: Okay. Okay, I'll see what I can do.

CHARLA: Really?

ELLEN: I'll check into tickets.

CHARLA: Great.

(CHARLA happily releases ELLEN's strings.

ADAM sneaks into the schoolyard. He heads to the wall, takes out a chalk and starts drawing a large picture on the back wall, the beginning of an eagle. It's a very fine, realistic depiction.

CHARLA enters and watches.)

ADAM: What're you lookin' at?

CHARLA: What you're drawing.

ADAM: I wasn't drawin' nothin'.

CHARLA: Okay.

ADAM: You tell anybody it was me, I'll grind your teeth in the sidewalk.

CHARLA: Don't worry.

ADAM: You're the one who's worried. You're the one who's gonna get her house burned down.

CHARLA: I won't tell.

ADAM: Better pray you don't.

CHARLA: … What's it gonna be?

ADAM: What's what gonna be?

CHARLA: Nothing.

ADAM: You're smart.

> *(He pushes her and runs off.*
> *PAIGE enters.)*

PAIGE: Hi, Charla. Guess what?

CHARLA: What?

PAIGE: We made a decision.

CHARLA: About what?

PAIGE: The group.

CHARLA: What did you decide?

PAIGE: We decided … not to let you in.

CHARLA: Oh.

PAIGE: Disappointed?

CHARLA: Not really.

PAIGE: I'm sorry, Charla, but you know how it is. So many kids want to get in, we can't take everybody.

CHARLA: I know.

PAIGE: You're new, maybe in a couple of months we'll have room for you.

CHARLA: *(Crushed.)* Maybe next year.

PAIGE: I don't believe it! Oh come on, Charla, don't you have a sense of humour? I was kidding!

CHARLA: You were?

PAIGE: Yeah. We decided—you're in!

CHARLA: Really?

(PAIGE lets CHARLA squirm again for a moment.)

PAIGE: Of course you are! Unless you don't want to.

CHARLA: *(Quickly.)* I do.

PAIGE: Sure?

CHARLA: Yeah.

PAIGE: And that means you're invited to Micky's party.

CHARLA: I am?

PAIGE: Gonna go?

CHARLA: *(Delighted.)* For sure.

PAIGE: What're you gonna wear?

CHARLA: I don't know.

PAIGE: It's gonna be a really great party, you gotta look really great.

CHARLA: I guess I should get something.

PAIGE: Me too. Want to go shopping tomorrow?

CHARLA: Where?

PAIGE: The mall, where else?

CHARLA: Okay, that'd be great.

(JOSH enters. He watches CHARLA, wanting to talk to her.)

PAIGE: What does he want?

CHARLA: I don't know.

PAIGE: God, he's such a loser, he gives me the creeps … Get lost, Josh.

(JOSH moves away a little, but keeps watching CHARLA.)

CHARLA: Don't be mean to him, Paige.

PAIGE: He's looking at you. I think he's got a crush on you.

CHARLA: No, he doesn't.

PAIGE: He's in love with you.

CHARLA: He is not.

PAIGE: Do you love him?

CHARLA: No.

PAIGE: Then tell him to get lost.

CHARLA: Why?

PAIGE: I told you, he gives me the creeps.

CHARLA: Where's he supposed to go?

PAIGE: Somewhere away from us. Unless you'd rather be with him.

CHARLA: No.

PAIGE: Then tell him. Go on.

CHARLA: I don't want to.

PAIGE: I thought you wanted to do stuff, go shopping, go to Micky's party.

CHARLA: I do.

PAIGE: It's up to you, Charla.

> *(Pause. CHARLA looks at JOSH.)*

CHARLA: *(Softly.)* Get lost.

> *(JOSH doesn't move.)*

PAIGE: I don't think he heard you.

CHARLA: … Get lost.

> *(JOSH looks at her, hurt. He moves away, against the wall.)*

PAIGE: He listened to you. He is in love with you. Come on, let's go.

> *(PAIGE starts to move off. CHARLA hesitates, looking at JOSH.)*

Are you coming?

> *(CHARLA, upset, follows.*
>
> *JOSH watches her go.*
>
> *End of Act One.)*

Act Two

(The four kids sit in front of their TVs, each holding a remote, scanning the channels. As they change the channels, we hear snips of TV dialogue. It is spoken as voice-over by the kids.)

ADAM: Spread 'em! You have the right to remain silent.

PAIGE: Don't have a cow, Dad.

ADAM: Doooe!

(Laughter.)

CHARLA: *(Sings.)* [Totally cool, totally hot, totally hair Barbie!]

PAIGE: And remember: No glove, no love.

JOSH: Do you love me? Say you love me?

ADAM: *(Sings.)* [I'm a Bud Man, that's what I am …]

CHARLA: The following programme contains mature subject matter and may not be suitable for children.

JOSH: [It keeps going and going and going and going …]

CHARLA: Do you love me? Say you love me!

JOSH: I made a million dollars, so can you!

ADAM: [Now you're playing with power.]

CHARLA: Nuns with bad habits—on the next [A Current Affair].

(JOSH sings the theme to [Jeopardy].)

PAIGE: Kids and guns. Report at eleven.

CHARLA: Don't touch me, don't come near me.

ADAM: *(Sings.)* [Bad boys, bad boys! Whatcha gonna do, whatcha gonna do when they come for you?]

PAIGE: Do you love me? Say you love me!

CHARLA: So who's paying the child support, the dog?

>   *(Laughter.)*

ADAM: Real life. Real drama. Real TV.

PAIGE: Even after showering I don't feel completely fresh.

JOSH: *(Sings.)* [You got the right one baby …]

ALL: [… Uh huh!]

CHARLA: Leave me alone, I'm having a bad day.

ADAM: Do you love me? Say you love me!

PAIGE: [Don't just hide 'em, oxy-cute 'em!]

JOSH: Mom, Dad, I love you.

ALL: Awwww …

>   *(They click off their TVs and move off.*
>   *CHARLA and PAIGE are at the mall. PAIGE is carrying several*
>   *bags of stuff.)*

PAIGE: What do you think of this top?

CHARLA: I love it, it's perfect.

PAIGE: The colour's wrong.

CHARLA: I like it.

PAIGE: Then why don't you try it on?

CHARLA: It's too expensive.

PAIGE: No it's not.

CHARLA: I've only got ten bucks.

PAIGE: What can you get for ten bucks?

CHARLA: I was hoping for a sale.

PAIGE: Good luck.

>   *(They move to another space.)*

>   Oh, [The Body Shop], I love this place, come on.

>   *(PAIGE checks the bottles.)*

>   Smell this.

CHARLA: Oh that's nice.

PAIGE: Orange cream bath. It makes your skin feel so good. My Mom
buys it by the gallon.

CHARLA: *(Picking one up.)* They have little bottles too.

PAIGE: Oh, too bad, twelve bucks.

CHARLA: *(Putting it back.)* There's hardly anything in it.

PAIGE: But it's worth it. I love their eye cream, don't you?

CHARLA: Never tried it.

PAIGE: You should, otherwise your eyes'll get wrinkled and you'll need a million face lifts like [Cher]. I mean, I can understand one or two, but she's worse than [Michael Jackson]. Should I get a nose job?

CHARLA: Why?

PAIGE: It's slightly crooked. See?

CHARLA: No.

PAIGE: You can't see it in this light. Look from this angle.

CHARLA: I can only sort of see it.

PAIGE: You must be blind. It's disgustingly bent. Not quite as bad as yours, but bad, you know what I mean? Are you going to get yours done?

CHARLA: I don't know. Is it expensive?

PAIGE: Yeah, I think so. My mom's cost as much as a mortgage payment. But her nose is perfect now. Maybe we can find you something at the [Thrifty's] sale.

CHARLA: Okay.

> *(CHARLA slowly follows.*
>
> *JOSH sombrely watches television as he works on a new magic trick.)*

TV: And now Video Magicians! Take the wand, tap your head three times …

> *(JOSH drops the stick. He picks up the TV remote and listlessly spins through the stations.*
>
> *BILL, his father the phone, enters.)*

BILL: Hey, look who's home!

JOSH: Hi, Dad.

BILL: *(Trying to cheer JOSH up.)* What's the trick for today?

JOSH: No trick.

BILL: Oh, come on, make a coin disappear.

JOSH: I don't feel like it.

BILL: Got a present for you.

JOSH: You did? What?

BILL: The story of the greatest magician who ever lived.

JOSH: Houdini?

BILL: Houdini.

(He gives JOSH a book.)

(Warmly.) He could escape anything: Handcuffs, straight jackets, they'd chain him up and sink him in the water and a minute later he'd be free. Nothing could stop Houdini, not even death.

(The phone rings. He answers it.)

Yeah, what?

JOSH: Dad—

BILL: Hold, son ... *(Into the phone.)* Did they accept the offer? No? Those fools will pay big for it!

(He hangs up.)

JOSH: Houdini would swell his muscles and the handcuffs would just drop off.

BILL: Good advice, son.

(He dials the phone.)

Swell the estimate! We'll bump 'em up till they drop right off!

(He smiles at JOSH.)

Thanks, Josh!

JOSH: You're welcome.

(BILL winks at him and exits.

JOSH looks in the book.)

Houdini: Buried alive in the water torture cell.

(CHARLA enters sadly.

ELLEN, the marionette, enters.)

CHARLA: What are you doing home so early?

ELLEN: I told my boss I wouldn't work overtime again. I had to say something, it's not worth working there if he treats me badly.

CHARLA: Did you get the tickets for the football game yet?

ELLEN: I'm sorry, I didn't have a chance. I will. What did you get at the mall?

CHARLA: Nothing!

ELLEN: I thought you were going to buy a new top.

CHARLA: I was. But what are you supposed to get for ten bucks?

ELLEN: I don't know, that's all we can afford right now.

CHARLA: I found one top for the ten bucks. I tried it on. Nobody could stop laughing.

ELLEN: Who was laughing?

CHARLA: Everybody.

ELLEN: Is Paige everybody?

CHARLA: She had her mom's credit card. She went to [Club Monaco] and got the greatest top and the most excellent skirt. She looked like [Vogue] magazine. She gets everything she wants, looks great all the time. Why can't I have anything?

ELLEN: I'm sorry, but we don't have that kind of money.

CHARLA: Yeah, I know!

ELLEN: But you don't need that stuff too look good. You're really beautiful.

CHARLA: No I'm not.

ELLEN: Of course you are.

CHARLA: I'm ugly. My nose is all huge and crooked. My teeth stick out. I've got ears like a dog.

ELLEN: That's not true. None of that is true.

CHARLA: I need a good outfit for Micky's party.

ELLEN: It's hard, Charla, your Dad hasn't sent the money he promised.

CHARLA: Well when it comes, can I go shopping? I know the top I want, it's at the [Gap]—

ELLEN: We'll see.

CHARLA: … Let's call him.

ELLEN: Why?

CHARLA: To see if he sent the money yet.

ELLEN: Not right now, Charla.

CHARLA: Why not?

ELLEN: It's a long distance call. It's expensive.

CHARLA: I want to go to the football game.

(CHARLA storms off.)

ELLEN: Charla—Charla!

(She struggles to follow, but the marionette operator controlling her exits, taking her in the opposite direction.

ADAM sneaks to the wall. He looks around, then continues his drawing of the eagle. Suddenly he freezes.

NYTRO appears.)

NYTRO: Hey, punk.

(ADAM keeps drawing.)

You.

(ADAM turns.)

ADAM: Talking to me?

NYTRO: Who else?

ADAM: How can I help you, Mr. Nytro sir.

NYTRO: I'm looking for something.

ADAM: Like what?

NYTRO: My brother's bike. He's very upset.

ADAM: Oh. Where did he put it?

NYTRO: It was locked up. Some very sad person took it.

ADAM: Why are they sad?

NYTRO: They're not sad yet. But they will be soon.

ADAM: I'll keep my eyes open. You'll be the first to know.

NYTRO: Good ... were you the one?

ADAM: Me? I wouldn't touch your brother's bike.

NYTRO: No. You wouldn't. Because you know how disappointed I would be if it was you.

ADAM: It's not me.

NYTRO: And you know what happens when I'm disappointed.

ADAM: I know.

NYTRO: Exactly?

(His arm raises.)

ADAM: I know, I know!

NYTRO: Good. Did you eat breakfast this morning?

ADAM: No.

NYTRO: Not good. Eat breakfast.

ADAM: I will. Okay!

(NYTRO goes. ADAM watches him leave.

School bell rings.

CHARLA enters.)

CHARLA: Paige!

PAIGE: Have you seen Micky?

CHARLA: No. Not yet.

PAIGE: I thought he'd be here by now.

CHARLA: I've got something for you.

PAIGE: What is it?

CHARLA: Wish bracelet.

PAIGE: Did you make it or buy it?

CHARLA: Made it. Can I put it on you?

PAIGE: Sure.

(CHARLA does.)

CHARLA: Are you making a wish?

PAIGE: I made fifty wishes.

CHARLA: You only get one.

PAIGE: Not too tight. You're stopping my circulation!

CHARLA: Sorry.

PAIGE: You better take it off. I don't want to get a blood disease.

CHARLA: Okay.

PAIGE: It's very pretty, Charla, thank you.

CHARLA: You're welcome. I can make you another one.

PAIGE: That's okay, I should probably only wear the ones Micky gives me anyway.

(PAIGE gives the bracelet back to CHARLA.)

CHARLA: Right.

PAIGE: So did you think of something for the group to do on the weekend?

CHARLA: Yes, I have lots of ideas.

PAIGE: You do? Great! Let's hear them.

CHARLA: Well, first I thought the Planetarium.

PAIGE: The what?

CHARLA: The Planetarium.

PAIGE: That's like school. Why would we want to go there on the weekend?

CHARLA: There's a laser show and music.

PAIGE: At the Planetarium? Charla, no offence intended, but the Planetarium is totally boring. What other ideas did you have?

CHARLA: We could go to a movie.

PAIGE: A movie, great! Which one?

CHARLA: How about the new [Robin Williams]?

PAIGE: Haven't you seen it yet?

CHARLA: No.

PAIGE: Oh. I've seen it about five times. What else?

CHARLA: The art gallery.

PAIGE: Huh?

CHARLA: They're having a big exhibition of whale paintings.

PAIGE: I didn't know whales could paint.

CHARLA: It's paintings *of* whales.

PAIGE: I knew that. It was a joke. I guess we'll just have to go to the mall. I like your jacket. How much was it?

CHARLA: It was my Mom's.

PAIGE: Oh.

CHARLA: But I really like it.

PAIGE: You better, you're wearing it.

>   *(MICKY walks by.)*

>   Micky!

>   *(He waves nervously and exits.)*

>   I've got a great idea for the party!

>   *(PAIGE exits.*

>   *CHARLA examines the bracelet.*

>   *JOSH enters with the silk handkerchief over his head. CHARLA goes to JOSH.)*

CHARLA: Why do you have that on?

JOSH: This is a silk of invisibility.

CHARLA: Then why can I see you?

(JOSH peeks out.)

JOSH: Because I am allowing you to.

CHARLA: I'm sorry I was mean to you before.

JOSH: I don't remember.

CHARLA: I told you to get lost.

JOSH: That's possible.

CHARLA: Well I'm sorry.

JOSH: If it happens again you will pay big.

CHARLA: I promise never to do it again.

JOSH: Then you are forgiven.

CHARLA: Thank you.

(She feels his handkerchief.)

It's nice, it's silk.

JOSH: The best ones are made of silk. This one is most certainly a man-made substance. Silk derives from moths that eat mulberry leaves.

CHARLA: Moths make silk?

JOSH: No, the moths eat the leaves. It's their children that make the silk … Would you like to learn how to become invisible?

CHARLA: Sure.

JOSH: First you must learn the incantation.

CHARLA: Okay.

JOSH: Incastapa quo bohanti.

CHARLA: Incastapa quo …

JOSH: Bohanti.

CHARLA: Bohanti.

JOSH: Good. Now take the wand, tap your head, say the words, and cover yourself.

CHARLA: Incastapa quo bohanti!

(She covers herself.)

Did it work?

JOSH: Ummm. Yes.

CHARLA: Am I really invisible?

JOSH: I can't see you.

CHARLA: Then how come I can see myself?

JOSH: Because you're invisible. That proves it.

CHARLA: Come on, you can see me.

(JOSH looks for CHARLA, feeling the air.)

JOSH: Where are you? Charla! Charla!

CHARLA: Right here!

JOSH: Be careful you don't get run over, nobody can see you.

CHARLA: Josh.

JOSH: Hey, Charla.

CHARLA: Hey, Josh?

JOSH: How do you feel about living the rest of your life like this?

CHARLA: I wasn't planning on it.

JOSH: But I don't know how to reverse the formula.

(CHARLA takes off the silk.)

CHARLA: Get outta here!

JOSH: I can see you, guess the spell wore off.

CHARLA: Guess so.

(JOSH grabs the silk and puts it over his head.)

Josh—

(CHARLA sees that ADAM has entered.

ADAM goes straight to JOSH.)

ADAM: Hey, Josh, how goes it? Howya doin'?

(ADAM starts dragging JOSH around with the cloth still on his head.)

Are you playing ghost? Are you a tablecloth?

CHARLA: Leave him alone!

ADAM: Get lost, Charcoal Head! Josh and me are taking a trip around the world.

(ADAM swings JOSH faster and faster. CHARLA goes for ADAM.)

CHARLA: Stop it!

ADAM: You want him? He's all yours!

(ADAM lets JOSH fly into CHARLA. They both go down. CHARLA removes the silk.)

Oh, yeah, Joshy, where's the money you owe me?

CHARLA: He doesn't owe you anything.

ADAM: Do you got it?

JOSH: I—

(ADAM collars JOSH.)

ADAM: Give it to me!

(They hear NYTRO approaching.

ADAM freezes. He lets JOSH go and runs off.

NYTRO appears.)

NYTRO: I want that punk. Adaaaaam!

(NYTRO exits, chasing ADAM. They watch NYTRO go.)

CHARLA: What do you think he'll do to Adam?

JOSH: He will filet him like a fish and remove every bone from his body.

CHARLA: Think Adam'll leave you alone now?

JOSH: I don't think so.

(ADAM, breathless, runs to the door of his house. He looks around fearfully, pounds on the door.)

ADAM: Ma!

(The door opens and ADAM enters the house.)

Mom.

(Adam's mother, a CAT, appears. She is very affectionate.)

CAT: Adam, are you alright?

ADAM: Yeah, I just—

CAT: You're hot.

(ADAM sits down.)

ADAM: Sick. Teacher sent me home from school.

CAT: All out of breath.

ADAM: Not feelin' so good.

CAT: You should rest.

ADAM: Okay.

CAT: You should watch some TV.

ADAM: Thanks, Mom.

> *(He turns on the TV.*
>
> *ADAM's father, a DOG, appears. Growling, he looks ADAM over.)*

DOG: What are you doin' home?

ADAM: I'm sick.

DOG: *(Sniffing him.)* You don't look sick to me.

ADAM: Don't feel good.

DOG: *(Pushing him.)* Get back to school.

ADAM: I can't.

DOG: You're lying.

ADAM: I am not.

> *(DOG knocks ADAM down.)*

ADAM's mother and father, a CAT and a DOG, fight.

DOG: Yes you are!

CAT: Stop it.

DOG: What?

CAT: He's not well.

DOG: You baby him.

CAT: He needs me.

DOG: He needs to grow up.

> *(CAT hisses. DOG growls. And it builds into a full fledged DOG and CAT fight.*
>
> *As the fight continues, ADAM runs out. He goes under the house, blocks his ears as the barking and yowling peaks.*
>
> *Lights come up on MISHA, who sings as he rips up some papers.)*

MISHA: It's a beautiful day in the neighbourhood, a neighbourly day in this neighbour-wood. ... You be my ... Would you be my ... neighbour?

> *(PAIGE enters.)*

PAIGE: What are you doing in my room?

MISHA: This is Mr. Roger's neighbourhood.

PAIGE: This is my room and you're making a mess.

MISHA: No, I'm making snow. I'm a snowblower!

> *(MISHA throws the torn up papers in the air.)*

PAIGE: You better clean this all up.

> *(PAIGE examines the papers he's ripping.)*

This paper's got writing on it. It's a letter from Micky. These are all my notes and letters from Micky. You wrecked them all!

MISHA: I did not! I made snow.

PAIGE: These are my letters! You came in my room and tore up my mail!

MISHA: Oops!

PAIGE: I hate you!

> *(PAIGE hits MISHA. MISHA howls.*
>
> *Paige's MOM enters.)*

MOM: What's going on up there?

MISHA: Paige hit me!

MOM: Paige!

PAIGE: He busted in my room without permission and tore up my letters from Micky!

MOM: From Micky? Oh, Misha!

PAIGE: You brat!

MISHA: *(Crying.)* I'm no brat, I'm a snowblower!

MOM: Oh, Misha, don't cry.

MISHA: I think my arm is broke.

MOM: Paige, can't you just leave him alone?

PAIGE: Me leave *him* alone?

MOM: He is three years old, Paige, you're twelve and a half.

PAIGE: So?

> *(DAD enters.)*

DAD: So act your age.

PAIGE: Just keep him out of my room.

MOM: We all have to help, Paige.

PAIGE: Why doesn't someone help me for a change?

> *(MISHA throws more paper.)*

MISHA: It's snowing!

PAIGE: Get out of my room!

DAD: Can't you control your daughter?

MOM: Paige, please.

PAIGE: What did I do?

DAD: I heard you went shopping. How'd you pay for it?

PAIGE: Mom gave me her credit card.

DAD: I thought we agreed no more charges till we pay off the account.

MOM: Relax, it's just a little outfit. It cost pennies.

DAD: It all adds up. Let's see the receipt.

MOM: Paige.

> *(PAIGE reaches into her bag and gives him the receipt.)*

DAD: Pennies? She spent ninety five bucks!

MOM: You're kidding.

> *(She looks.)*

My god, Paige, what's wrong with you?

PAIGE: You've been to that store, you know how much it costs.

MOM: I didn't say you could break the bank. I can't believe how irresponsible you are.

DAD: She's going to have to take it back.

PAIGE: But you promised.

MOM: Take it back.

PAIGE: But the party.

DAD: Take it back right now.

> *(DAD exits.*
> *MOM hands PAIGE the receipt.*
> *MISHA throws up more paper.)*

MISHA: It's snowing!

MOM: Mama's little snowblower. Come to Mommy!

PAIGE's mother and father, a car and a mannequin.

MISHA: Snow!

> (*He jumps in her arms and as they go, MISHA turns to PAIGE and laughs devilishly. They exit. PAIGE sadly picks up the scraps of paper.*
>
> *Lights come up on CHARLA, holding the bracelet. She's not very happy.*
>
> *ELLEN enters. She is no longer a marionette, now she is played by the actress who operated the marionette, in a similar costume, with strings attached to her arms and legs. Operators hold her strings from the top of the wall.*)

ELLEN: God, I can't believe how late it is, have you been here long?

CHARLA: Since three-thirty.

ELLEN: I'm sorry, I had to do the shopping, get the car fixed.

CHARLA: Forget it.

ELLEN: I'll start dinner, you must be starving.

CHARLA's mother, the marionette, comes alive.

CHARLA: I'm not hungry.

ELLEN: You've got to eat.

CHARLA: Did you go to get the tickets for the game?

ELLEN: Yeah, I went. Did you see the big pot?

CHARLA: Where are they, let me see them!

ELLEN: They're not here. Look, I'm starting dinner.

CHARLA: I thought you went to pick them up.

ELLEN: I did. I can't find the rice.

CHARLA: So where are they?

ELLEN: I couldn't afford them.

CHARLA: You promised.

ELLEN: They were twenty five dollars a ticket.

CHARLA: So?

ELLEN: I'm worried about the rent, Charla.

CHARLA: You said you'd take me, just like Dad used to take me.

ELLEN: He still hasn't sent the money he promised.

(CHARLA pulls on ELLEN's strings.)

CHARLA: It wasn't my idea to move to this stupid city. It wasn't my idea for you and Dad to split up!

ELLEN: Look, I'm sorry, just let me finish making dinner and—

CHARLA: It's not fair!

(CHARLA sits alone, disconsolate.)

ELLEN: Forget dinner! Charla!

(She rips off the strings holding her and goes to CHARLA.)

I'm sorry, honey. I'm sorry it's so hard.

CHARLA: Me too.

ELLEN: But I'm trying. I really am.

CHARLA: I know.

ELLEN: Look, I'll get the tickets. We'll find a way.

CHARLA: That's okay. I know they're expensive. We can do something else.

ELLEN: … Like what?

CHARLA: How about the art gallery? There's a big exhibition of whale
  paintings.

ELLEN: Really?

CHARLA: Yeah. I bet you didn't know whales could paint.

>*(ELLEN hugs CHARLA. They exit.*
>
>*JOSH enters. He sits and opens his Houdini book.*
>
>*MICKY enters. Looks around. JOSH, puzzled, looks up from his
book. MICKY adjusts his collar.)*

JOSH: What?

>*(MICKY slowly approaches JOSH. Pause.)*

What did I do?

>*(MICKY reaches into his pocket and gives JOSH a note.)*

For me?

MICKY passes a note to JOSH. On the wall behind them is ADAM's
drawing of an eagle.

(MICKY indicates "No." JOSH looks at the note.)

It's for Paige? You want me to give this to Paige?

(MICKY indicates "Yes" enthusiastically.)

Okay, if that's what you want.

(MICKY pats JOSH on the back.)

I'll do it, I'll do it.

(MICKY gives JOSH a thumb's up. JOSH pockets the note and goes back to his book.

CHARLA enters.)

CHARLA: What're you reading?

JOSH: The biography of Harry Houdini.

CHARLA: Who's he?

JOSH: He was the greatest magician and escape artist who ever lived. He had the strongest stomach muscles in the world. And that's how he died.

CHARLA: How?

JOSH: A student in Montreal punched Houdini in the stomach before he could tighten his muscles. Broke his appendix and he bled to death inside.

CHARLA: That's horrible.

JOSH: The man who punched him bragged that he was stronger than Houdini.

CHARLA: But he wasn't, he cheated.

JOSH: Houdini swore he'd come back. He'd be reincarnated in the form of a young magician.

CHARLA: Do you think that you—

(JOSH shrugs, wonderingly.)

JOSH: Houdini could do anything.

CHARLA: Wow.

(PAIGE enters.)

PAIGE: Charla, have you seen Micky?

CHARLA: No.

JOSH: I …

PAIGE: What, Josh?

JOSH: I …

PAIGE: Josh, do us a both a favour and go back to your book. Improve your mind. You need it.

(JOSH sits back down with his book.)

I don't know what could have happened to him. Do you think he might be seeing somebody behind my back?

CHARLA: I don't know.

PAIGE: I was looking through my little mirror in class today and saw Allison M smiling at him. And he was smiling back.

CHARLA: People smile at each other all the time.

PAIGE: Not like that. I saw how they were smiling. But she'd have to be pretty stupid to try and steal Micky from me. Not with her eyeballs.

CHARLA: What's wrong with her eyeballs?

PAIGE: Oh, come on, Charla, don't pretend you haven't noticed them. Allison M has abnormal eyeballs.

CHARLA: I never noticed.

PAIGE: Well, look in the mirror, you'll see 'em. Your eyeballs are just ever-so-slightly deformed. It's some kind of birth defect.

CHARLA: Paige, there is nothing wrong with my eyes so quit putting me down.

PAIGE: I wasn't putting you down, Charla, we're friends. I'm just trying to help.

CHARLA: Sure.

PAIGE: With a little make-up, it wouldn't even be noticeable.

CHARLA: What kind of make-up?

JOSH: Excuse me, I—

PAIGE: Get lost, Josh!

CHARLA: Leave him alone, what'd he do to you?

PAIGE: He interrupted my train of thought.

JOSH: But I—

PAIGE: Charla, tell him to get lost!

CHARLA: No way.

PAIGE: You will if you want to stay in the group.

(CHARLA looks at JOSH. Beat.)

CHARLA: I don't care about your stupid group.

PAIGE: Well then, you're out, Charla. And you're never getting back in.

CHARLA: What makes you so great, Paige?

PAIGE: So you have been talking to Allison M.

CHARLA: No I haven't.

PAIGE: Yes you have. She hates me 'cause I kicked her out of the group. And now she's turned you against me.

CHARLA: That's not true.

PAIGE: You don't have to lie. I know the kind of things you're saying behind my back. I tried to be nice to you Charla but you obviously don't know how to appreciate a friend.

JOSH: This is for you!

(JOSH hands the note to PAIGE and sits down again.)

PAIGE: What is this, Josh? Don't you have anything better to do?

(She looks at the note, opens it and reads it. She is upset. Pause.)

CHARLA: What's wrong, Paige?

PAIGE: Forget it.

CHARLA: What happened?

(PAIGE passes her the note.)

PAIGE: He broke up with me. He wants me to give his ring to Allison M. I knew it.

(Beat.)

It doesn't matter, I was gonna break up with him anyway.

CHARLA: You were?

PAIGE: Yes, of course, he bugs me. Who wants to go to his stupid party anyway? Besides, he kisses funny and he has halitosis.

CHARLA: Really?

PAIGE: Yes. Allison M better buy a gas mask ... What are you staring at? My eyebrows?

CHARLA: No.

PAIGE: Don't lie to me, you can see them. Everybody can see them.

CHARLA: See what?

PAIGE: How they grow together like a caveman's.

CHARLA: You have totally normal eyebrows.

PAIGE: Then why doesn't [Claudia Schiffer] have eyebrows like mine?

CHARLA: Because she's a model and pulls them out!

PAIGE: I do too but they keep growing back, blacker and thicker.

CHARLA: Maybe they're supposed to be there.

PAIGE: No way. I should get electrolysis. Stick needles in at the bottom of each hair, one by one and electrocute the roots.

CHARLA: That's gross.

PAIGE: I bet [Claudia Schiffer] electrocutes her eyebrows.

CHARLA: There's nothing wrong with your eyebrows. Why do you want to look like somebody else?

(PAIGE considers the question.

ADAM furtively runs on with the bike.)

ADAM: I gotta get rid of this. You gotta help me.

CHARLA: No way. You stole that.

ADAM: Nytro's coming. He's gonna kill me.

PAIGE: My heart bleeds for you, Adam.

ADAM: I'll pound all your faces in. I'll cut your feet off. Help me!

CHARLA: Why don't you go to the principal's office?

ADAM: I'll get suspended. And then my Dad'll get me.

CHARLA: Maybe not. Maybe she'll help you.

ADAM: It's too late. He's coming. I'm dead.

PAIGE: Too bad, Adam. You asked for it.

(ADAM shoves CHARLA and PAIGE.)

ADAM: Get away from me, both of you. You're scum. You'd watch a helpless man die.

(The girls move away.)

Help.

JOSH: Psst.

(ADAM looks.

JOSH motions him over.)

ADAM: What do you want?

JOSH: Would you like to disappear?

ADAM: Yes, that's exactly what I want.

JOSH: Look no further.

(JOSH pulls out his magic wand. He taps on his hand three times. He pulls the cloth out of his sleeve.)

ADAM: You're crazy.

JOSH: You are close to death. Do you wish to disappear?

ADAM: You can't make me disappear.

JOSH: Sit.

(ADAM sits. JOSH taps him once on the head with the wand.)

Incastapa quo bohanti.

(And he throws the cloth over ADAM's head.)

ADAM: Did it work?

JOSH: Shh!

(JOSH looks up.

NYTRO enters.)

NYTRO: I saw that punk come this way.

JOSH: You mean Adam?

NYTRO: Yeah.

JOSH: I think he is being suspended.

NYTRO: Good.

JOSH: I believe that his father is grinding his bones into dust as we speak.

NYTRO: Glad to hear it.

JOSH: He asked me to give back your brother's bike.

NYTRO: There it is. Any scratches?

JOSH: It is in perfect condition. I will gladly guard it until your brother picks it up.

NYTRO: Thank you.

JOSH: Adam begs you for forgiveness and swears that he has learned his lesson and will never steal your little brother's bike again.

NYTRO: Or I'll squash him till green stuff runs outta his ears.

JOSH: I'll be sure to tell him.

NYTRO: See ya kid. Remember, always eat broccoli.

JOSH: Okay, Nytro. Bye.

(Slight pause. NYTRO goes.

CHARLA and PAIGE run up to JOSH.)

CHARLA: That was great, Josh.

PAIGE: How'd you do that?

CHARLA: You were fantastic!

JOSH: It was not me. It was Harry Houdini, the greatest escape artist of all time.

CHARLA: I think I believe you.

(They turn and look at ADAM, covered in the cloth and cowering.)

PAIGE: You can come out now, Adam.

ADAM: Is he gone?

CHARLA: The coast is clear.

ADAM: Am I really invisible?

PAIGE: I don't think so.

(ADAM peeks out.)

ADAM: Then why didn't he see me?

JOSH: Magic.

PAIGE: Aren't you gonna thank him, Adam?

CHARLA: You owe Josh your life.

(Pause.

ADAM throws the silk at JOSH. Then he runs to the wall and starts to work on the eagle drawing.

The school bell rings.)

PAIGE: Josh, give me your honest opinion: Should I get my eyebrows electrocuted?

JOSH: Even if you electrocute them, they will grow back, so you have to electrocute them again and again.

PAIGE: Eyebrows are just like [Freddy Kruger].

CHARLA: Yeah.

JOSH: Yes.

CHARLA: Hey, Josh, do you want to see the new [Robin Williams] movie?

JOSH: ... Sure.

PAIGE: Haven't you seen it?

JOSH: No. But now I will.

(JOSH exits.

PAIGE exits.

CHARLA carefully goes over to ADAM.)

CHARLA: I found this.

(She takes out the note he gave PAIGE and shows it to him.)

ADAM: So?

CHARLA: It's yours.

ADAM: What about it?

CHARLA: You draw really well.

ADAM: You wanna get your face smashed in?

CHARLA: Not really. I just like your picture, that's all.

(Pause.)

ADAM: Then you keep it.

CHARLA: Okay.

ADAM: Okay.

(CHARLA goes.

ADAM watches her exit, then he finishes the eagle. It comes off the wall, flaps its wings, and soars away.

The End.)